Poems of the Seasons

PICTURES BY
GORDON BENINGFIELD

Viking

VIKING

Published by the Penguin Group
Penguin Books Ltd, 27 Wrights Lane, London W8 5TZ, England
Penguin Books USA Inc., 375 Hudson Street, New York, New York 10014, USA
Penguin Books Australia Ltd, Ringwood, Victoria, Australia
Penguin Books Canada Ltd, 10 Alcorn Avenue, Toronto, Ontario, Canada M4V 3B2
Penguin Books (NZ) Ltd, 182-190 Wairau Road, Auckland 10, New Zealand

Penguin Books Ltd, Registered Offices: Harmondsworth, Middlesex, England

First published 1992
1 3 5 7 9 10 8 6 4 2

Pictures copyright © Gordon Beningfield 1978, 1980, 1983, 1985, 1987, 1988, 1989, 1990, 1992
Design copyright © Cameron Books 1992

Selected by Jill Hollis
Designed by Jill Hollis and Ian Cameron

Produced by Cameron Books, P.O.Box 1, Moffat, Dumfriesshire DG10 9SU, Scotland

Filmset in New Baskerville by Cameron Books
Printed in the Netherlands by Royal Smeets Offset, Weert

A CIP catalogue record for this book is available from the British Library

ISBN 0-670-84546-9

Thanks are due for their permission to reproduce copyright material in this volume: to Mrs
Nicolete Gray and the Society of Authors on behalf of the Laurence Binyon Estate for
'Early June', 'Harebell and Pansy', and extracts from 'Strange Fruit' and 'Thunder on the
Downs' by Laurence Binyon; to Peters Fraser & Dunlop Ltd for extracts from 'The Gift: for
CMP' and 'Wilderness, and to Carcanet Press Ltd for 'What is Winter?' by Edmund
Blunden from Selected Poems ed. Robyn Marsack; to Rosemary Seymour for 'Sudden Spring'
by Gerald Bullett; to the Estate of Richard Church for 'A Procession' by Richard Church; to
the Literary Executor of Leonard Clark for 'Christmas' by Leonard Clark; to the Literary
Trustees of Walter de la Mare and The Society of Authors as their representative for
'Martins: September' by Walter de la Mare; to the Estate of Robert Frost for 'Reluctance'
from The Poetry of Robert Frost ed. E.C. Lathem, published by Jonathan Cape; to the
Enitharmon Press for 'St Luke's Summer' by Phoebe Hesketh; to Faber and Faber Ltd for
'April Birthday' by Ted Hughes; to Peters Fraser & Dunlop Ltd for 'April Rise' and 'Cock
Pheasant' by Laurie Lee; to Curtis Brown, London, for 'Fritillaries', an extract from The
Land copyright 1947 Vita Sackville-West; to Alison Young (© The Andrew Young Estate) for
'A Windy Day' by Andrew Young. Cameron Books has made every effort to obtain
permission to reproduce material in copyright and apologises to any copyright holder who
has proved impossible to contact.

Pictures

Poems

The Seasons
from *The Art of Preserving Health*

Observe the circling year, how unperceiv'd
Her seasons change! behold! by slow degrees,
Stern winter turn'd into a ruder spring;
The ripen'd spring a milder summer glows;
Departing summer sheds Pomona's store;
And aged autumn brews the winter storm.

JOHN ARMSTRONG (170-9-1779)

The Snowdrop

Yes, punctual to the time, thou'rt here again,
As still thou art: though frost or rain may vary,
And icicles blockade the rockbirds' aery,
Or sluggish snow lie heavy on the plain,
Yet thou, sweet child of hoary January,
Art here to harbinger the laggard train
Of vernal flowers, a duteous missionary.
Nor cold can blight, nor fog thy pureness stain.
Beneath the dripping eaves, or on the slope
Of cottage garden, whether mark'd or no,
Thy meek head bends in undistinguish'd row.
Blessings upon thee, gentle bud of hope!
And Nature bless the spot where thou dost grow—
Young life emerging from thy kindred snow!

HARTLEY COLERIDGE (1796-1849)

To a Snowdrop

Lone flower, hemm'd in with snows, and white as they,
But hardier far, once more I see thee bend
Thy forehead, as if fearful to offend,
Like an unbidden guest. Though day by day,
Storms, sallying from the mountain-tops, waylay
The rising sun, and on the plains descend:
Yet art thou welcome, welcome as a friend
Whose zeal outruns his promise! Blue-eyed May
Shall soon behold this border thickly set
With bright jonquils, their odours lavishing
On the soft west wind and his frolic peers:
Nor will I then thy modest grace forget,
Chaste Snowdrop, venturous harbinger of Spring,
And pensive monitor of fleeting years!

WILLIAM WORDSWORTH (1770-1850)

Snowdrop

Could you understand
One who was wild as if he found a mine
Of golden guineas, when he noticed first
The soft green streaks in a Snowdrop's inner leaves?

ROBERT BUCHANAN (1841-1901)

Harbingers of Spring

For Snowdrops are the harbingers of Spring,
A sort of link between dumb life and light,
Freshness preserved amid all withering,
Bloom in the midst of grey and frosty blight,
Pale Stars that gladden Nature's dreary night!

CAROLINE ELIZABETH NORTON (1808-1877)

14

The Unloosening

Winter was weary. All his snows were failing—
Still from his stiff gray head he shook the rime
Upon the grasses, bushes and broad hedges,
But all was lost in the new touch of Time.

And the bright-globèd hedges were all ruddy,
As though warm sunset glowed perpetual.
The myriad swinging tassels of first hazel,
From purple to pale gold, were swinging all

In the soft wind, no more afraid of Winter.
Nor chaffinch, wren, nor lark was now afraid.
And Winter heard, or (ears too hard of hearing)
Snuffed the South-West that in his cold hair played.

And his hands trembled. Then with voice a-quaver
He called the East Wind, and the black East ran,
Roofing the sky with iron, and in the darkness
Winter crept out and chilled the earth again.

And while men slept the still pools were frozen,
Mosses were white, with ice the long grasses bowed;
The hawthorn buds and the greening honeysuckle
Froze, and the birds were dumb under that cloud.

And men and beasts were dulled, and children even
Less merry, under that low iron dome.
Early the patient rooks and starlings gathered;
Any warm narrow place for men was home.

And Winter laughed, but the third night grew weary,
And slept all heavy, till the East Wind thought him dead.
Then the returning South West in his nostrils
Breathed, and his snows melted. And his head

Uplifting, he saw all the laughing valley,
Heard the unloosened waters leaping down
Broadening over the meadows; saw the sun running
From hill to hill and glittering upon the town.

All day he stared. But his head drooped at evening,
Bent and slow he stumbled into the white
Cavern of a great chalk hill, hedged with tall bushes,
And in its darkness found a darker night

Among the broken cliff and falling water,
Freezing, or falling quietly everywhere;
Locked in a long, long sleep, his brain undreaming,
With only water moving anywhere.

Old men at night dreamed that they saw him going,
And looked, and dared not look, lest he should turn.
And young men felt the air beating on their bodies,
And the young women woke from dreams that burn.

And children going through the fields at morning
Saw the unloosened waters leaping down,
And broke the hazel boughs and wore the tassels
Above their eyes—a pale and shaking crown.

JOHN FREEMAN (1880-1929)

The Falling Night

Shepherds all, and maidens fair,
Fold your flocks up, for the air
'Gins to thicken, and the sun
Already his great course hath run.
See the dew-drops, how they kiss
Every little flower that is.
Hanging on their velvet heads,
Like a rope of crystal beads:
See the heavy clouds low falling,
And bright Hesperus down calling
The dead Night from under ground;
At whose rising, mists unsound,
Damps and vapours fly apace,
Hovering o'er the wanton face
Of these pastures, where they come,
Striking dead both bud and bloom:
Therefore, from such danger lock
Every one his lovèd flock;

And let your dogs lie loose without,
Lest the wolf come as a scout
From the mountain, and ere day,
Bear a lamb or kid away;
Or the crafty thievish fox
Break upon your simple flocks.
To secure yourselves from these,
Be not too secure in ease;
Let one eye his watches keep,
Whilst the other eye doth sleep;
So you shall good shepherds prove,
And for ever hold the love
Of our great god. Sweetest slumbers,
And soft silence fall in numbers
Of our eyelids! So, farewell!
Thus I end my evening's knell.

JOHN FLETCHER (1579-1625)

The New-Drop'd Lamb

Ah, gentle shepherd, thine the lot to tend,
Of all that feel distress, the most assailed,
Feeble, defenceless: lenient be thy care;
But spread around thy tend'rest diligence
In flow'ry spring-time, when the new-drop'd lamb,
Tott'ring with weakness by his mother's side,
Feels the fresh world about him; and each thorn,
Hillock, or furrow, trips his feeble feet.
O guard his meek sweet innocence from all
Th' innum'rous ills, that rush around his life;
Mark the quick kite, with beak and talons prone,
Circling the skies to snatch him from the plain;
Observe the lurking crows, beware the brake,
There the fly fox the careless minute waits;
Nor trust thy neighbour's dog, nor earth nor sky,
Thy bosom to a thousand cares divide.
Eurus oft slings his hail; the tardy fields
Pay not their promis'd food; and oft the dam
O'er her weak twins with empty udder mourns,
Or fails to guard, when the bold bird of prey
Alights, and hops in many turns around,
And tires her also turning: to her aid
Be nimble, and the weakest, in thine arms,
Gently convey to the warm cote, and oft,
Between the lark's note and the nightingale's,
His hungry bleating still with tepid milk;
In this office may thy children join;
And charitable habits learn in sport.

JOHN DYER (1699-1757)

The Primrose

Though storms may break the Primrose on its stalk,
Though frosts may blight the freshness of its bloom,
Yet Spring's awakening breath will woo the earth
To feed with kindliest dews its favourite flower,
That blooms in mossy banks and darksome glens,
Lighting the greenwood with its sunny smile,
Fear not then, Spirit, Death's disrobing hand.

PERCY BYSSHE SHELLEY (1792-1822)

Spring Flowers

The loveliest flowers the closest cling to earth,
And they first feel the sun; so violets blue,
So the soft star-like primrose drenched in dew,
The happiest of Spring's happy, fragrant birth,
To gentlest touches sweetest tones reply;—
Still humbleness with her low-breathed voice
Can steal o'er man's proud heart, and win his choice
From earth to heaven, with mightier witchery
Than eloquence or wisdom e'er could own.
Bloom on then in your shade, contented bloom,
Sweet flowers, nor deem yourselves to all unknown,
Heaven knows you, who one day for their altered doom
Shall thank you, taught by you to abase themselves and live.

JOHN KEBLE (1792-1866)

To an Early Primrose

Mild offspring of a dark and sullen sire!
Whose modest form, so delicately fine,
Was nursed in whirling storms,
And cradled in the winds.

Thee, when young spring first questioned Winter's sway,
And dared the sturdy blusterer to the fight,
Thee on this bank he threw
To mark his victory.

In this low vale, the promise of the year,
Serene, thou openest to the nipping gale,
Unnoticed and alone,
Thy tender elegance.

So virtue blooms, brought forth amid the storms
Of chill adversity; in some lone walk
Of life she rears her head,
Obscure and unobserved;

With every bleaching breeze that on her blows
Chastens her spotless purity of breast,
And hardens her to bear
Serene the ills of life.

HENRY KIRKE WHITE (1785-1806)

21

The Miracle

Come, sweetheart, listen, for I have a thing
Most wonderful to tell you—news of Spring.
Albeit Winter still is in the air
And the Earth troubled, and the branches bare,
Yet down the fields to-day I saw her pass—
The Spring—her feet went shining through the grass,
She touched the ragged hedgerows—I have seen
Her finger-prints, most delicately green;
And she has whispered to the crocus leaves,
And to the garrulous sparrows in the eaves.
Swiftly she passed and shyly, and her fair
Young face was hidden in her cloudy hair.
She would not stay, her season is not yet,
But she has reawakened, and has set
The sap of all the world astir, and rent
Once more the shadows of our discontent.
Triumphant news—a miracle I sing—
The everlasting miracle of Spring.

JOHN DRINKWATER (1882-1937)

Ploughing up the Pasture

Now up the pasture's slope the ploughed land laps
In folds that fall and crumble from the share
Rooks drop to the warm earth, hot leather creaks,
The sweat of labouring flesh steams in the air,
The flanks of beast are smooth with sun and toil,
The cropped turves that are worn with years of grazing
Turn inwards to the steel, and over the long
Acres of grassland stretch the ribs of soil.
No longer when in summer the clotted shadows
Fall from the crest of trees, will they stretch over
The lazy turf, but will shadow a new world
Of yellow acres, fret and stir of meadows,
Green barley, freckled silver by the wind.
And corn like a fresh sea across the world.

MARGARET STANLEY-WRENCH (20th century)

On Ploughing

The slow shuttle of husbandry
Has plodded up and down
Till folds of tilth are lying
In ripples of shining brown.

The slow thoughts of my ancestry
Are moving across my brain,
Turning today's deeds under,
Laying the old facts plain:

How my father strode at his furrowing,
My mother's father spun
And worked in the mills of weaving;
So the image of both is one . . .

The plough, horses and harnessing
Weaving slow lines of thread:
My grandfather and my father
Sweating for daily bread.

EVELYN D. BANGAY (20th century)

To the Small Celandine

Pansies, lilies, kingcups, daisies,
Let them live upon their praises;
Long as there's a sun that sets,
Primroses will have their glory;
Long as there are Violets,
They will have a place in story:
There's a flower that shall be mine,
'Tis the little Celandine.

Eyes of some men travel far
For the finding of a star;
Up and down the heavens they go,
Men that keep a mighty rout!
I'm as great as they, I trow,
Since the day I found thee out,
Little Flower!—I'll make a stir,
Like a great astronomer.

Modest, yet withal an Elf
Bold, and lavish of thyself;
Since we needs must first have met
I have seen thee, high and low,
Thirty years or more, and yet
'Twas a face I did not know;
Thou has now, go where I may,
Fifty greetings in a day.

Ere a leaf is on a bush,
In the time before the Thrush
Has a thought about her nest,
Thou wilt come with half a call,
Spreading out thy glossy breast
Like a careless Prodigal;
Telling tales about the sun,
When we've little warmth, or none.

Poets, vain men in their mood!
Travel with the multitude:
Never heed them; I aver
That they all are wanton wooers;
But the thrifty Cottager,
Who stirs little out of doors,
Joys to spy thee near her home;
Spring is coming, Thou are come!

Comfort have thou of thy merit,
Kindly unassuming Spirit!
Careless of thy neighbourhood,
Thou dost show thy pleasant face
On the moor, and in the wood,
In the lane—there's not a place,
Howsoever mean it be,
But 'tis good enough for thee.

Ill befall the yellow Flowers,
Children of the flaring hours!
Buttercups, that will be seen,
Whether we will see or no;
Others, too, of lofty mien;
They have done as worldlings do,
Taken praise that should be thine,
Little, humble Celandine!

Prophet of delight and mirth,
Ill-requited upon earth;
Herald of a mighty band,
Of a joyous train ensuing,
Serving at my heart's command,
Tasks that are no tasks renewing,
I will sing, as doth behove,
Hymns in praise of what I love!

WILLIAM WORDSWORTH (1770-1850)

April Birthday

When your birthday brings the world under your window
  And the song-thrush sings wet-throated in the dew
And aconite and primrose are unsticking the wrappers
  Of the package that has come today for you

      Lambs bounce out and stand astonished
      Puss willow pushes among bare branches
      Sooty hawthorns shiver into emerald

And a new air
      Nuzzles the sugary
      Buds of the chestnut. A groundswell and a stir
      Billows the silvered
      Violet silks
      Of the south—a tenderness
      Lifting through all the
      Gently-breasted
      Counties of England.

When the swallow snips the string that holds the world in
  And the ring-dove claps and nearly loops the loop
You just can't count everything that follows in the tumble
  Like a whole circus tumbling through a hoop

      Grass in a mesh of all flowers floundering
      Sizzling leaves and blossoms bombing
      Nestling hissing and groggy-legged insects

And the trees
      Stagger, they stronger
      Brace their boles and biceps under
      The load of gift. And the hills float
      Light as bubble glass
      On the smoke-blue evening

And rabbits are bobbing everywhere, and a thrush
Rings coolly in a far corner. A shiver of green
Strokes the darkening slope as the land
Begins her labour.

TED HUGHES (b 1930)

April

April, April,
Laugh thy girlish laughter;
Then, the moment after,
Weep thy girlish tears!
April, that mine ears
Like a lover greetest,
If I tell thee, sweetest,
All my hopes and fears,
April, April,
Laugh thy golden laughter,
But, the moment after,
Weep thy golden tears!

JOHN WILLIAM WATSON (1858-1935)

from *The Passionate Shepherd*

The fields are green, the spring grows on apace,
  And Nature's art begins to take the air;
Each herb her scent, each flower doth show her grace,
  And beauty braggeth of her bravest fair.
The lambs and rabbits sweetly run at base;
  The fowls do plume, and fishes fall to play;
The muses all have chose a sitting place
  To sing and play the shepherd's roundelay . . .
The little wren that never sung a note
  Is peeping now to prove how she can sing;
The nightingale hath set in tune her throat,
  And all the woods with little robins ring . . .
Love is abroad as naked as my nail,
  And little birds do flicker from their nests;
Diana sweet hath set aside her veil,
  And Phillis shows the beauty of her breasts.
O blessëd breasts, the beauty of the spring!
  O blessëd spring, that such a beauty shows!
Of highest trees the holly is the king,
  And of all flowers fair fall the queen, the rose!

NICHOLAS BRETON (?1553-?1625)

April Rise

If ever I saw blessing in the air
  I see it now in this still early day
Where lemon-green the vaporous morning drips
  Wet sunlight on the powder of my eye.

Blown bubble-film of blue, the sky wraps round
  Weeds of warm light whose every root and rod
Splutters with soapy green, and all the world
  Sweats with the bead of summer in its bud.

If ever I heard blessing it is there
  Where birds in trees that shoals and shadows are
Splash with their hidden wings and drops of sound
  Break on my ears their crests of throbbing air.

Pure in the haze the emerald sun dilates,
  The lips of sparrows milk the mossy stones,
While white as water by the lake a girl
  Swims her green hand among the gathered swans.

Now as the almond burns its smoking wick,
  Dropping small flames to light the candled grass;
Now, as my low blood scales its second chance,
  If ever world were blessed, now it is.

LAURIE LEE (b 1914)

Sudden Spring

Spring is sudden: it is her quality.
However carefully we watch for her,
However long delayed
The green in the winter'd hedge
The almond blossom
The piercing daffodil,
Like a lovely woman late for her appointment
She's suddenly here, taking us unawares,
So beautifully annihilating expectation
That we applaud her punctual arrival.

GERALD BULLETT (1893-1958)

By A Brook

Townsmen, or of the hamlet, young or old,
Whithersoever you may wander now,
Where'er you roam from, would you waste an hour,
Or sleep thro' one brief dream upon the grass, —
Pause here. The murmurs of the rivulet,
Rippling by cressy isles or bars of sand,
Are pleasant from the early Spring to when,
Full fields of barley shifting tearful lights
On growing spears, by fits the lady ash
With twinkling fingers sweeps her yellow keys.

ALFRED, LORD TENNYSON (1809-1892)

Winter Violets

Death-white azaleas watched beside my bed,
And tried to tell me tales of Southern lands;
But they in hothouse air were born and bred,
And they were gathered by a stranger's hands:
They were not sweet, they never have been free,
And all their pallid beauty had no voice for me.

And all I longed for was one common flower
Fed by soft mists and rainy English air,
A flower that knew the woods, the leafless bower
The wet, green moss, the hedges sharp and bare—
A flower that spoke my language, and could tell
Of all the woods and ways my heart remembers well.

Then came your violets—and at once I heard
The sparrows chatter on the dripping eaves
The full stream's babbling inarticulate word,
The plash of rain on big wet ivy leaves;
I saw the woods where thick the dead leaves lie,
And smelt the fresh earth's scent—the scent of memory.

The unleafed trees—the lichens green and grey,
The wide sad-coloured meadows, and the brown
Fields that sleep now, and dream of harvest day
Hiding their seeds like hopes in hearts pent down—
A thousand dreams, a thousand memories
Your violets' voices breathed in unheard melodies—

Unheard by all but me. I heard, I blessed
The little English, English-speaking things
For their sweet selves that laid my wish to rest,
For their sweet help that lent my dreaming wings,
And, most of all, for all the thoughts of you
Which make them smell more sweet than any other violets do.

EDITH NESBIT (1858-1924)

There's Many a Flower

The crocus flaunts its beauty in the sun;
The palm-fragrance greets us from afar;
The daisy shines as bright as any star;
The bluebell splashes woods while brake is dun;
With woof of green pale primrose-light is spun;
Black heaths are patched with coltsfoot-gold bizarre,
The snowdrop strews the fields like mottled spar;
The social daffodil hails every one—
All these do meet the rambler's careless eye
Unsought for, but the violet's sweet smile
Lies hidden, like a gem from vulgar pry,
'Mid lushest dew-beds, safe from all the glare
Of noons; first guerdon of all those who dare,
Mid Spring's caprices, wander mile on mile.

WILLIAM DOWSING (19th-early 20th century)

To Violets

Welcome, maids of honour,
You do bring
In the Spring
And wait upon her.

She has virgins many,
Fresh and fair
Yet you are
More sweet than any.

You're the maiden posies,
And so graced
To be placed
'Fore damask roses.

Yet, though thus respected
By and by
Ye do lie,
Poor girls, neglected.

ROBERT HERRICK (1591-1674)

A Violet
from *Hamlet*

A violet in the youth of primy nature,
Forward, not permanent, sweet, not lasting,
The perfume and suppliance of a minute;
No more.

WILLIAM SHAKESPEARE (1564-1616)

The Violet and the Rose

The violet in the wood, that's sweet to-day,
Is longer sweet than roses of red June;
Set me sweet violets along my way,
And bid the rose flower, but not too soon.
Ah violet, ah rose, why not the two?
Why bloom not all fair flowers the whole year through?
Why not the two, young violet, ripe rose?
Why dies one sweetness when another blows

AUGUSTA WEBSTER (1837-1894)

Nesting Birds

Of birds, how each, according to her kind,
Proper materials for her nest can find;
And build a frame, which deepest thought in man
Would or amend, or imitate in vain?
How in small flights they know to try their young,
And teach the callow child her parent's song?
Why these frequent the plain, and those the wood?
Why ev'ry land has her specific brood?
Where the tall crane, or wandr'ing swallow goes,
Fearful of gathering winds and falling snows?
If into rocks or hollow trees they creep,
In temporary death confin'd to sleep.
Or conscious of the coming evil, fly
To milder regions, and a southern sky?

MATTHEW PRIOR (1664-1721)

The Voice of Spring

See the yellow catkins cover
All the slender willows over;
And on banks of mossy green
Star-like primroses are seen;
And, their clustering leaves below,
White and purple violets blow.

Hark! the new-born lambs are bleating,
And the cawing rooks are meeting
In the elms—a noisy crowd;
All the birds are singing loud;
And the first white butterfly
In the sunshine dances by.

Look around thee—look around!
Flowers in all the fields abound;
Every running stream is bright;
All the orchard trees are white;
And each small and waving shoot
Promises sweet flowers and fruit.

Turn thine eyes to earth and heaven
God for thee the spring has given,
Taught the birds their melodies,
Clothed the earth, and cleared the skies,
For thy pleasure or thy food—
Pour thy soul in gratitude!

MARY HOWITT (1799-1888)

from *A Year's Windfalls*

In the wind of windy March
    The catkins drop down,
Curly, caterpillar-like,
    Curious green and brown.
With concourse of nest-building birds
    And leaf-buds by the way,
We begin to think of flowers
    And life and nuts some day.

CHRISTINA ROSSETTI (1830-1894)

from *Misconceptions*

This is a spray the Bird clung to,
  Making it blossom with pleasure,
Ere the high tree-top she sprung to,
  Fit for her nest and her treasure.
  Oh, what a hope beyond measure
      Was the poor spray's, which the flying feet hung to,—
      So to be singled out, built in, and sung to!

ROBERT BROWNING (1812-1889)

from *'I Stood Tip-toe Upon a Little Hill'*

I gazed awhile, and felt as light, and free
As though the fanning wings of Mercury
Had played upon my heels: I was light-hearted,
And many pleasures to my vision started;
So I straightway began to pluck a posey
Of luxuries bright, milky, soft, and rosy.
A bush of May-flowers with the bees about them,
And let long grass grow round the roots to keep them
Moist, cool and green; and shade the violets
That they may bind the moss in leafy nets.

JOHN KEATS (1795-1821)

Description of Spring
Wherein Each Thing Renews, Save only the Lover

The sootë* season, that bud and bloom forth brings   *sweet
With green hath clad the hill, and eke the vale:
The nightingale with feathers now she sings;
The turtle to her mate hath told her tale;
Summer is come, for every spray now springs,
The hart hath hung his old head on the pale;
The buck in brake his winter coat he flings;
The fishes float with now repaired scale;
The adder all her slough away she slings;
The swift swallow pursueth the flies smale*;   *small
The busy bee her honey now she mings*;   *mingles
Winter is worn that was the flowers' bale.
  And thus I see among these pleasant things,
  Each care decays, and yet my sorrow springs.

HENRY HOWARD (?1517-1547)

The Flowering May-Thorn Tree

There stands the flowering May-thorn tree!
From through the veiling mist you see
The black and shadowy stem;
Smit by the sun, the mist in glee
Dissolves to lightsome jewel'ry,
Each blossom hath its gem.

SAMUEL TAYLOR COLERIDGE (1772-1834)

from *A Defence of English Spring*

. . . As yet but single,
The bluebells with the grasses mingle;
But soon their azure will be scrolled
Upon the primrose cloth-of-gold.
Yes, those are early lady-smocks,
The children crumple in their frocks,
And carry many a zig-zag mile,
O'er meadow, footpath, gate, and stile
To stick in pots and jugs to dress
Their cottages sills and lattices.

ROBERT BRIDGES (1844-1930)

from *The May Queen*

The honeysuckle round the porch has wov'n its bowers,
And by the meadow-trenches blow the faint sweet cuckoo-flowers;
And the wild marsh marigold shines like fire in swamps and hollows gray,
And I'm to be Queen o' the May, mother, I'm to be Queen o' the May.

ALFRED, LORD TENNYSON (1835-1913)

Fritillaries

But once I went through the lanes, over the sharp
Tilt of the little bridges; past the forge,
And heard the clang of anvil and iron,
And saw the founting sparks in the dusky forge,
And men outside with horses, gossiping.
So I came through that April England, moist
And green in its lush fields between the willows,
Foaming with cherry in the woods, and pale
With clouds of lady's-smock along the hedge,
Until I came to a gate and left the road
For the gentle fields that entice me, by the farms,
Wandering through the embroidered fields each one
So like its fellow; wandered through the gaps,
Past the mild cattle knee-deep in the brooks,
And wandered drowsing as the meadows drowsed
Under the pale wide heaven and slow clouds.
And then I came to a field where the springing grass
Was dulled by the hanging cups of fritillaries,
Sullen and foreign-looking, the snaky flower,
Scarfed in dull purple, like Egyptian girls
Camping among the furze, staining the waste
With foreign colour, sulky—dark and quaint,
Dangerous too, as a girl might sidle up,
An Egyptian girl, with an ancient snaring spell,
Throwing a net, soft round the limbs and heart,
Captivity soft and abhorrent, a close-meshed net,
—See the square web on the murrey flesh of the flower—
Holding her captive close with her bare brown arms.

VICTORIA SACKVILLE-WEST (1892-1962)

Evening Orchard

All the beauty of the world
    Fading white,
All Spring's beauty, Summer's sweet,
    Wanton heat,
Wantoning 'neath the narrow bosom
    Of starry-flowered
Apple tree in late May blossom.

All the sweetness of the world
    Wanton White,
Paling cheek and fading heat,
    Wasting hue,
Stars the tree's thin breast with flower
    Like white stars
Shaken from sky-arching bower.

All the beauty, all the sweetness
    Staying white:
The ruddy gone, the brief pink gone,
    And bridal light
Shining yet while grasses flush
    With evening's gold,
And Eden's is the orchard thrush.

JOHN FREEMAN (1880-1929)

from *A Year's Windfalls*

With the gusts of April
    Rich fruit-tree blossom fall,
On the hedged-in orchard-green,
    From the southern wall.
Apple-trees and pear-trees
    Shed petals white or pink,
Plum-trees and peach-trees;
    While sharp showers sink and sink.

CHRISTINA ROSSETTI (1830-1894)

from *The Seasons*

…And see the country, far diffus'd around,
One boundless blush, one white impurpled shower
Of mingled blossoms; where the raptur'd eye
Hurries from joy to joy.

JAMES THOMSON (1700-1748)

from *Song of the Bluebells*

Sweet bluebells we,
Mid flowers of the lea,
The likest in hue to heaven
Our bonnets so blue
Are tinged with the dew
That drops from the sky at even.

Our bloom more sweet
Than dark violet,
Or tulip's purple stain,
At every return
Of the dew-breathing morn,
Grows brighter and brighter again.

GEORGE DARLEY (1795-1846)

from *Bluebells*

Tonight from deeps of loneliness I wake in wistful wonder
To a sudden sense of brightness, an immanence of blue—
O are there bluebells swaying in the shadowy coppice yonder,
Shriven with the dawning and the dew?

LUCIA C. MARKHAM (late 19th-early 20th century)

Bluebells

'One day, one day, I'll climb that distant hill
    And pick the bluebells there!'
So dreamed the child who lived beside the rill
And breathed the lowland air.
    'One day, one day when I am old I'll go
And climb the mountain where the bluebells blow.'

'One day! one day!' The child was now a maid,
    A girl with laughing look;
She and her lover sought the valley-glade
Where sang the silver brook.
    'One day,' she said, 'love, you and I will go
And reach that far hill where the bluebells blow!'

Years passed. A woman now with wearier eyes
    Gazed towards that sunlit hill.
Tall children clustered round her. How time flies!
The bluebells blossomed still.
    She'll never gather them! All dreams fade so.
We live and die, and still the bluebells blow.

GEORGE BARLOW (19th century)

46

On a Bed of Forget-me-nots

I love its growth at large and free
By untrod path and unlopped tree,
Or nodding by the unpruned hedge,
Or on the water's dangerous edge
Where flags and meadowsweet blow rank
With rushes on the quaking bank.

CHRISTINA ROSSETTI (1830-1894)

from *The Keepsake*

Nor can I find, amid my lonely walk
By rivulet, or spring, or wet roadside,
That blue and bright-eyed floweret of the brook,
Hope's gentle gem, the sweet Forget-me-not.

SAMUEL TAYLOR COLERIDGE (1772-1834)

from *On May Morning*

The little blue Forget-me-not
Comes too on friendship's gentle plea,
Spring's messenger in every spot,
Smiling on all,— 'Remember me!'

JOHN CLARE (1793-1864)

from *Auguries of May*

The sedge-wren tells her note,
    Dim larks in ether float,
The uprolled clouds sustain their pageant dome.
    In velvet, sunshine-fed,
    Spires up the bulrush head,
Where rock the wild swans in their reedy home.

    The lily pale and wan
    Puts all her glories on:
Her silver mantle and her golden crest.
    The humbler violets stand
    Her ladies at command,
As she attires in lawn her ivory breast.

JOHN BYRNE LEICESTER WARREN (1835-1895)

from *The Gift: for C.M.P.*

The mill-wheel, cheerful drudge, would roll
And splash and drum, but the bright-eyed vole
Would never care for him, would swim
Across his racing waves, and slim
Sharp dace would watch in the quickest gush,
And forget-me-not and flag and rush
Would take up quarters there, boom as he might.

EDMUND BLUNDEN (1896-1974)

The Mood of May

When May is in his prime, then may each heart rejoice:
When May bedecks each branch with green, each bird strains forth his voice.
The lively sap creeps up into the blooming thorn;
The flowers, which cold in prison kept, now laugh the frost to scorn.
All nature's imps triumph whiles joyful May doth last;
When May is gone, of all the year the pleasant time is past.

May makes the cheerful hue, May breeds and brings new blood;
May marcheth throughout every limb, May makes the merry mood.
May pricketh tender hearts their warbling notes to tune:
Full strange it is, yet some we see do make their May in June.
Thus things are strangely wrought whiles joyful May doth last;
Take May in time, when May is gone the pleasant time is past.

All ye that live on earth, and have your May at will,
Rejoice in May, as I do now, and use your May with skill.
Use May while that you may, for May hath but his time,
When all the fruit is gone, it is too late the tree to climb.
Your liking and your lust is fresh whiles May doth last;
When May is gone, of all the year the pleasant time is past.

RICHARD EDWARDS (1524-1566)

At the Close of Spring

The garlands fade that Spring so lately wove,
  Each simple flower which she had nursed in dew,
Anemones that spangled every grove,
  The primrose wan, and hare-bell mildly blue.
No more shall violets linger in the dell,
  Or purple orchis variegate the plain,
Till Spring again shall call forth every bell,
  And dress with humid hands her wreaths again.
Ah! poor humanity! so frail, so fair,
  Are the fond visions of thy early day,
Till tyrant passion and corrosive care
  Bid all thy fairy colours fade away!
Another May new buds and flowers shall bring;
Ah! why has happiness no second Spring?

CHARLOTTE SMITH (1749-1806)

Early June

Spring's over, over. The gold meadows tarnish,
The gold dims, heavy-leaved hedges darken,
The primal light diminishes.
I look, look back, and hearken
Now but to faint and ever fainter echoes.
Summer lays siege, and Spring's brief fire finishes.

Never was such a glory as this Spring glory,
Never a cloudy navy of such brightness
Moving all day to nights serener.
But I, who shared that lightness,
Feel already the season's weight more sombre,
Already the leaves falling, and the brave boughs grown leaner.

LAURENCE BINYON (1869-1943)

To the Dandelion

Dear common flower, that grow'st beside the way,
Fringing the dusty road with harmless gold,
First pledge of blithesome May,
Which children pluck, and full of pride uphold,
High-hearted buccaneers, o'erjoyed that they
An Eldorado in the grass have found,
Which not the rich earth's ample round
May match in wealth! Thou art more dear to me
Than all the prouder summer blooms may be.

Gold such as thine ne'er drew the Spanish prow
Through the primeval hush of Indian seas,
Nor wrinkled the lean brow
Of age, to rob the lover's heart of ease;
'Tis the Spring's largess, which she scatters now
To rich and poor alike, with lavish hand,
Though most hearts never understand
To take it at God's value, but pass by
The offered wealth with unrewarded eye.

Thou art my tropics and mine Italy;
To look at thee unlocks a warmer clime;
The eyes thou givest me
Are in the heart, and heed not space or time:
Not in mid June the golden-cuirassed bee
Feels a more summer-like warm ravishment
In the white lily's breezy tent,
His fragrant Sybaris, than I when first
From the dark green thy yellow circles burst.

Then think I of deep shadows on the grass,
Of meadows where in sun the cattle graze,
Where, as the breezes pass,
The gleaming rushes lean a thousand ways,
Of leaves that slumber in a cloudy mass,
Or whiten in the wind, of waters blue
That from the distance sparkle through
Some woodland gap, and of a sky above,
Where one white cloud like a stray lamb doth move.

My childhood's earliest thoughts are linked with thee;
The sight of thee calls back the robin's song,
Who, from the dark old tree
Beside the door, sang clearly all day long;
And I, secure in childish piety,
Listened as if I heard an angel sing
With news from heaven, which he could bring
Fresh every day to my untainted ears
When birds and flowers and I were happy peers.

How like a prodigal doth nature seem,
When thou, for all thy gold, so common art!
Thou teachest me to deem
More sacredly of every human heart,
Since each reflects in joy its scanty gleam
Of heaven, and could some wondrous secret show,
Did we but pay the love we owe,
And with a child's undoubting wisdom look
On all these living pages of God's book.

JAMES RUSSELL LOWELL (1819-1891)

A Summer's Day

My Guardian, bear me on thy downy wing
To some cool shade, where infant flowers spring,
Where on the trees sweet honeysuckles blow,
And ruddy daisies paint the ground below:
Where the shrill linnet charms the solemn shade,
And zephyrs pant along the cooler glade,
Or shake the bull-rush by a river-side,
While the gay sun-beams sparkle on the tide:
Oh! for some grot, whose rustic sides declare
Ease, and not splendour, was the builder's care;
Where roses feed their unaffected charms,
And the curl'd vine extends her clasping arms:
Where happy silence lulls the quiet soul,
And makes it calm as summer waters roll.
Here let me learn to check each growing ill,
And bring to reason disobedient will;

To watch this incoherent breast, and find
What fav'rite passions rule the giddy mind.
Here no reproaches grate the wounded ear;
We see delighted, and transported hear:
While the glad warblers wanton round the trees,
And the still waters catch the dying breeze.
Grief waits without, and melancholy gloom;
Come, chearful hope, and fill the vacant room;
Come, ev'ry thought, which virtue gave to please;
Come, smiling health! with thy companion, ease.
Let these, and all that virtue's self attends,
Bless the still hours of my gentle friends.
Peace to my foes, if any such there be,
And gracious heaven give kind repose to me.

MARY LEAPOR (1722-1746)

from *Ballad of Dowsabel*

This maiden in a morn betime,
Went forth when May was in the prime,
  To get sweet setywall,
The honey-suckle, the harlock
The lily, and the lady-smock,
  To deck her summer hall.

MICHAEL DRAYTON (1563-1631)

from *Gareth and Lynette*

Good Lord, how sweetly smells the honeysuckle
In the hush'd night, as if the world were one
Of utter peace, and love, and gentleness.

ALFRED, LORD TENNYSON (1809-1892)

Honeysuckle
from *Much Ado about Nothing*

And bid her steal into the pleached bower,
Where honeysuckles, ripen'd by the sun,
Forbid the sun to enter, like favourites,
Made proud by princes . . .

WILLIAM SHAKESPEARE (1564-1616)

To The Daisy

With little here to do or see
Of things that in the great world be,
Daisy! again I talk to thee,
   For thou art worthy,
Thou unassuming Common-place
Of Nature, with that homely face,
And yet with something of a grace
   Which love makes for thee!

Oft on the dappled turf at ease
I sit, and play with similes,
Loose types of things, through all degrees,
   Thoughts of thy raising:
And may a fond and idle name
I give to thee, for praise or blame,
As is the humour of the game,
   While I am gazing.

A nun demure of lowly port;
Or sprightly maiden, of Love's court,
In thy simplicity the sport
   Of all temptations;
A queen in crown of rubies drest;
A starveling in a scanty vest;
Are all, as seems to suit thee best,
   Thy appellations.

A little Cyclops with one eye
Staring to threaten and defy,
That thought comes next—and instantly
   The freak is over,
The shape will vanish—and behold
A silver shield with boss of gold,
That spreads itself, some faery bold
   In fight to cover!

I see thee glittering from afar—
And then thou art a pretty star;
Not quite so fair as many are
   In heaven above thee!
Yet like a star, with glittering crest,
Self-poised in air thou seem'st to rest;—
May peace come never to his nest,
   Who shall reprove thee!

Bright flower! for by that name at last,
When all my reveries are past;
I call thee, and to that cleave fast,
   Sweet silent creature!
Thou breath'st with me in sun and air,
Do thou, as thou art wont, repair
   My heart with gladness, and a share
   Of thy meek nature!

WILLIAM WORDSWORTH (1770-1850)

from *The Legend of Good Women*

The long day I shape me for to abide,
For nothing else, and I shall not lie,
But for to look upon the Daisie,
That well by reason men it call may
The Daisie, or else the Eye of the Day,
The empress and flowre of flowres all.

GEOFFREY CHAUCER (c.1342-1400)

from *The Eternity of Nature*

Trampled under foot,
The daisy lives and strikes its root
Into the lap of time; centuries may come
And pass away into the silent tomb,
And still the child, hid in the womb of time,
Shall smile and pluck them, when this simple rhyme
Shall be forgotten, like a churchyard and stone,
Or lingering lie, unnoticed and alone.

JOHN CLARE (1793-1864)

The Bee

The pedigree of honey
Does not concern the bee
A clover, any time, to him
Is aristocracy.

EMILY DICKINSON (1830-1886)

from *The Seasons*

Here their delicious task the fervent bees
In swarming millions tend; around, athwart,
Through the soft air the busy nations fly,
Cling to the bud, and with inserted tube
Suck its pure essence, its aetherieal soul;
And oft, with bolder wing, they soaring dare
The purple heath, or where the wild thyme grows,
And yellow load them with the luscious spoil.

JAMES THOMSON (1700-1748)

A Procession

Marvellous wings filled the morning:
The bourdon bee from grass
To grass heaved his brown sacks;
The butterfly battled with air,
Adorning her wings with light.
Beetles with armoured backs
Flashed steel and bronze so bright
That a king, it seemed, must pass
For the hordes of the orchard to stare,
Raise huzzah and buzz
With rustic gossamer wing,
Their acclamation thus
Catching sunshine, noon-sound,
Hay-height above the ground,
Though none quite glimpsed the king.

RICHARD CHURCH (1893-1972)

from *The Months*

Heavy is the green of the fields, heavy the trees
With foliage hang, drowsy the hum of bees
In the thund'rous air: the crowded scents lie low:
Thro' tangle of weeds the river runneth slow.

ROBERT BRIDGES (1844-1930)

The Careful Insect
from *Rural Sports*

The careful Insect 'midst his works I view
Now from the Flow'rs exhaust the fragrant Dew,
With golden Treasures load his little Thighs,
And steer his airy Journey through the Skies:
With liquid Sweets the waxen Cells distend,
While some 'gainst Hostile Drones their cave defend;
Others with sweets the waxen cells distend:
Each in the Toil a proper Station bears,
And in the little Bulk a mighty Soul appears.

JOHN GAY (1685-1732)

The Flitting

I've left my own old home of homes,
Green fields and every pleasant place;
The summer like a stranger comes,
I pause and hardly know her face.
I miss the hazel's happy green,
The blue bell's quiet hanging blooms,
Where envy's sneer was never seen,
Where staring malice never comes.

I miss the heath, its yellow furze,
Molehills and rabbit tracks that lead
Through beesom, ling, and teazel burrs
That spread a wilderness indeed;
The woodland oaks and all below
That their white powdered branches shield;
The mossy paths: the very crow
Croaked music in my native fields.

I sit me in my corner chair
That seems to feel itself at home,
And hear bird music here and there
From hawthorn hedge and orchard come.
I hear, but all is strange and new:
I sat on my old bench in June,
The sailing puddock's shrill 'peelew'
On Royce Wood seemed a sweeter tune.

I walk adown the narrow lane,
The nightingale is singing now,
But like to me she seems at loss
For Royce Wood and its shielding bough.
I lean upon the window sill,
The bees and summer happy seem;
Green, sunny green they shine, but still
My heart goes far away to dream

Of happiness, and thoughts arise
With home-bred pictures many a one,
Green lanes that shut out burning skies
And old crook'd stiles to rest upon;
Above them hangs the maple tree,
Below grass swells a velvet hill,
And little footpaths sweet to see
Go seeking sweeter places still.

JOHN CLARE (1793-1864)

from *The Prelude*

Through quaint obliquities I might pursue
These cravings; when the foxglove, one by one,
Upwards through every stage of the tall stem,
Had shed beside the public way its bells,
And stood of all dismantled, save the last
Left at the tapering ladder's top, that seemed
To bend as doth a slender blade of grass
Tipped with a rain-drop . . .

WILLIAM WORDSWORTH (1770-1850)

from *Thyrsis*

So, some tempestuous morn in early June,
When the year's primal burst of bloom is o'er,
Before the roses and the longest day—
When garden-walks, and all the grassy floor,
With blossoms, red and white, of fallen May
And chestnut-flowers are strewn—
So have I heard the cuckoo's parting cry
From the wet field, through the vext garden-trees,
Come with the volleying rain and tossing breeze:
The bloom is gone, and with the bloom go I.

Too quick despairer, wherefore wilt thou go?
Soon will the high Midsummer pomps come on,
Soon will the musk carnations break and swell,
Soon shall we have gold-dusted snapdragon,
Sweet-William with its homely cottage-smell,
And stocks in fragrant blow;
Roses that down the alleys shine afar,
And open, jasmine-muffled lattices,
And groups under the dreaming garden-trees,
And the full moon, and the white evening-star.

MATTHEW ARNOLD (1822-1888)

Summer

Winter is cold-hearted,
   Spring is yea and nay,
Autumn is a weather-cock
   Blown every way:
Summer days for me,
When every leaf is on its tree:

When Robin's not a beggar,
   And Jenny Wren's a bride,
And larks hang singing, singing, singing,
   Over the wheat fields wide,
   And anchored lilies ride,
And the pendulum spider
   Swings from side to side.

And blue black beetles transact business,
   And gnats fly in a host,
And furry caterpillars hasten
   That no time be lost,
And moths grow fat and thrive,
And ladybirds arrive.

Before green apples blush,
   Before green nuts embrown,
Why, one day in the country
   Is worth a month in town:
   Is worth a day and a year
Of the dusty, musty, lag-last fashion
   That days drone elsewhere.

CHRISTINA ROSSETTI (1830-1894)

from *The Month of June*

It is the month of June
The month of leaves and roses,
When pleasant sights salute the eyes
And pleasant scents the noses.

NATHANIEL PARKER WILLIS (1806-1894)

To—

The roses make the world so sweet,
The bees, the birds have such a tune,
There's such a light and such a heat
And such a joy in June.

GEORGE MACDONALD (1824-1905)

Summer Night

I cannot see what flowers are at my feet,
　　Nor what soft incense hangs upon the boughs,
But in embalmed darkness, guess each sweet
　　Wherewith the seasonable month endows
The grass, the thicket, and the fruit-tree wild;
　　White hawthorn and the pastoral eglantine;
Fast-fasting violets cover'd up in leaves;
　　And mid-May's eldest child,
The coming musk-rose, full of dewy wine,
　　The murmurous haunt of flies on summer eves.

JOHN KEATS (1795-1821)

from *The Vision of Sir Launfal*

And what is so rare as a day in June?
Then, if ever, come perfect days;
Then Heaven tries earth if it be in tune,
And over it softly her warm ear lays;
Whether we look, or whether we listen,
We hear life murmur, or see it glisten;
Every clod feels a stir of might,
An instinct within it that reaches and towers,
And, groping blindly above it for light,
Climbs to a soul in grass and flowers;
The flush of life may well be seen
Thrilling back over hills and valleys;
The cowslip startles in meadows green,
The buttercup catches the sun in its chalice,
And there's never a leaf nor a blade too mean
To be some happy creature's palace;
The little bird sits at his door in the sun,
Atilt like a blossom among the leaves,
And lets his illumined being o'errun
With the deluge of summer it receives;
His mate feels the eggs beneath her wings,
And the heart in her dumb breast flutters and sings.
He sings to the wide world, and she to her nest,—
In the nice ear of Nature which song is the best?

JAMES RUSSELL LOWELL (1819-1891)

A Green Cornfield

'And singing still dost soar and soaring ever singest.'

The earth was green, the sky was blue:
  I saw and heard one sunny morn
A skylark hang between the two,
  A singing speck above the corn;

A stage below, in gay accord,
  White butterflies danced on the wing,
And still the singing skylark soared,
  And silent sank and soared to sing.

The cornfield stretched a tender green
  To right and left beside my walks;
I knew he had a nest unseen
  Somewhere among the million stalks.

And as I paused to hear his song
  While swift the sunny moments slid,
Perhaps his mate sat listening long,
  And listened longer than I did.

CHRISTINA ROSSETTI (1830-1894)

The Lark

The lark, that shuns on lofty boughs to build
Her annual nest, lies silent in the field.
But if the promise of a cloudless day,
Aurora smiling, bids her rise and play,
Then straight she shews, 'twas not for want of voice,
Or power to climb, she made so low a choice:
Singing she mounts, her airy wings are stretch'd
T'wards heav'n, as if from heav'n her notes she fetch'd.

EDMUND WALLER (1606-1687)

The Heaven-Soaring Lark

The heaven-soaring lark, its rapture spent
On morning's quest
Drops down again, soul satisfied, content
Unto the nest.

O singing soul, chafe not, that by earth's chain
Thou seemest bound!—
The sky's true messenger did ne'er disdain
The lowly ground.

MARY ELEANOR ROBERTS (late 19th-early 20th century)

Harebell and Pansy

O'er the round throat her little head
Its gay delight upbuoys:
A harebell in the breeze of June
Hath such melodious poise;
And chiming with her heart, my heart
Is only hers and joy's.

But my heart takes a deeper thrill,
Her cheek a rarer bloom,
When the sad mood comes rich as glow
Of pansies dipped in gloom.
By some far shore she wanders—where?
And her eyes fill—for whom?

LAURENCE BINYON (1869-1943)

The Harebell

. . .On the windy hills
Lo, the little harebell leans
On the spire-grass that it queens
With bonnet blue.

GEORGE MEREDITH (1828-1909)

from *The Prelude*

Or, not less pleased, lay on some turret's head,
Catching from tufts of grass and hare-bell flowers
Their faintest whisper to the passing breeze,
Given out, while mid-day heat oppressed the plains.

WILLIAM WORDSWORTH (1770-1850)

from *The Seasons*

Now, flaming up the heav'ns, the potent sun
Melts into limpid air the high rais'd clouds,
In partly colour'd bands; till wide unveil'd,
The face of nature shines, from where earth seems
Far stretched around, to meet the bending sphere.

JAMES THOMSON (1700-1748)

The Sun

The sun that rolls his beamy orbs on high,
Pride of the world and glory of the sky;
Illustrious in his course, in bright array
Marches along the heavenes, and scatters day
O'er earth, and o'er the main, and the etherial way.
He in the morn renews his radiant round,
And warms the fragrant bosom of the ground;
But e'er the noon of day, in fiery gleams
He darts the glory of his blazing beams;
Beneath the burnings of his sultry ray,
Earth to her centre pierced, admits the day;
Huge vales expand, where rivers roll'd before,
And lessen'd seas contract within their shore.

WILLIAM BROOME (1689-1745)

The Sun

The sun, like a golden knot on high,
Gathers the glories of the sky,
And binds them into a shining tent,
Roofing the world with the firmament.
And through the pavilion the rich winds blow,
And through the pavilion the waters go,
And the buds for joy, and the trees for prayer,
Bowing their heads in the sunny air . . .

GEORGE MACDONALD (1824-1905)

The Brook

Seated once by a brook, watching a child
Chiefly that paddled, I was thus beguiled.
Mellow the blackbird sang and sharp the thrush
Not far off in the oak and hazel bush,
Unseen. There was a scent like honeycomb
From mugwort dull. And down upon the dome
Of the stone the cart-horse kicks against so oft
A butterfly alighted. From aloft
He took the heat of the sun, and from below,
On the hot stone he perched contented so,
As if never a cart would pass again
That way; as if I were the last of men
And he the first of insects to have earth
And sun together and to know their worth.
I was divided between him and the gleam,
The motion, and the voices, of the stream,
The waters running frizzled over gravel,
That never vanish and for ever travel.
A grey flycatcher silent on a fence
And I sat as if we had been there since
The horseman and the horse lying beneath
The fir-tree-covered barrow on the heath,
The horseman and the horse with silver shoes,
Galloped the downs last. All that I could lose
I lost. And then the child's voice raised the dead.
'No one's been here before' was what she said
And what I felt, yet never should have found
A word for, while I gathered sight and sound.

EDWARD THOMAS (1878-1917)

Sky

. . . Look overhead
How air is azurëd;
O how! nay do but stand
Where you can lift your hand
Skywards: rich, rich it laps
Round the four fingergaps.
Yet such a sapphire-shot,
Charged, steepëd sky will not
Stain light. Yea, mark you this:
It does no prejudice.
The glass-blue days are those
When every colour glows,
Each shape and shadow shows.
Blue be it: this blue heaven
The seven or seven times seven
Hued sunbeam will transmit
Perfect, not alter it.
Or if there does some soft,
On things aloof, aloft,
Bloom breathe, that one breath more
Earth is the fairer for . . .

GERARD MANLEY HOPKINS (1844-1889)

from *Thunder on the Downs*

Wide earth, wide heaven, and in the summer air
Silence! The summit of the Down is bare
Between the climbing crests of wood; but those
Great sea-winds, wont, when the wet South-West blows,
To rock tall beeches and strong oaks aloud
And strew torn leaves upon the streaming cloud,
To-day are idle, slumbering far aloof.
Under the solemn height and gorgeous roof
Of cloud-built sky, all earth is indolent.
Wandering hum of bees and thymy scent
Of the short turf enrich pure loneliness;
Scarcely an airy topmost-twining tress
Of bryony quivers where the thorn it wreathes;
Hot fragrance from the honeysuckle breathes,
And sweet the rose floats on the arching briar's
Green fountains sprayed with delicate frail fires.

For clumps of thicket, dark beneath the blaze
Of the high westering sun, beset the ways
Of smooth grass narrowing where the slope runs steep
Down to green woods, and glowing shadows keep
A freshness round the mossy roots, and cool
The light that sleeps as in a chequered pool
Of golden air. O woods, I love you well,
I love the flowers you hide, your ferny smell;
But here is sweeter solitude, for here
My heart breathes heavenly space; the sky is near
To thought, with heights that fathomlessly glow;
And the eye wanders the wide land below.

And this is England! June's undarkened green
Gleams on far woods; and in the vales between
Gray hamlets, older than the trees that shade
Their ripening meadows, are in quiet laid,
Themselves a part of the warm, fruitful ground. . .

LAURENCE BINYON (1869-1943)

Poppies in the Wheat

Along Ancona's hills the shimmering heat,
A tropic tide of air, with ebb and flow
Bathes all the fields of wheat until they glow
Like flashing seas of green, which toss and beat
Around the vines. The poppies lithe and fleet
Seem running, fiery torchmen, to and fro
To mark the shore. The farmer does not know
That they are there. He walks with heavy feet,
Counting the bread and wine by autumn's gain,
But I—I smile to think that days remain
Perhaps to me in which, though bread be sweet
No more, and red wine warm my blood in vain,
I shall be glad remembering how the fleet,
Lithe poppies ran like torchmen with the wheat.

HELEN HUNT JACKSON (1830-1885)

from *The Poppy*

Summer set lip to earth's bosom bare,
And left the flushed print in a poppy there:
Like a yawn of fire from the grass it came,
And the fanning wind puffed it to flapping flame.

With burnt mouth, red like a lion's, it drank
The blood of the sun as he slaughtered sank,
And dipped its cup in the purpurate shine
When the eastern conduits ran with wine.

Till it grew lethargied with fierce bliss,
And hot as a swinkèd gipsy is,
And drowsed in sleepy savageries,
With mouth wide a-pout for a sultry kiss.

FRANCIS THOMPSON (1859-1907)

The Sheaves

Where long the shadows of the wind had rolled,
Green wheat was yielding to the change assigned,
And as by some vast magic undivined
The world was turning slowly into gold.
Like nothing that was ever bought or sold
It waited there, the body and the mind;
And with a mighty meaning of a kind
That tells the more the more it is not told.

So in a land where all days are not fair,
Fair days went on till on another day
A thousand golden sheaves were lying there,
Shining and still, but not for long to stay—
As if a thousand girls with golden hair
Might rise from where they slept and go away.

EDWIN ARLINGTON ROBINSON (1869-1935)

September 1815

While not a leaf seems faded; while the fields,
With ripening harvest prodigally fair,
In brightest sunshine bask; this nipping air,
Sent from some distant clime where Winter wields
His icy scimitar, a foretaste yields
Of bitter change, and bids the flowers beware;
And whispers to the silent birds, 'Prepare
Against the threatening foe your trustiest shields.'
To Nature's tuneful quire, this rustling dry
Through leaves yet green, and yon crystalline sky,
Announce a season potent to renew,
'Mid frost and snow, the instinctive joys of song,
And nobler cares than listless summer knew.

WILLIAM WORDSWORTH (1770-1850)

87

Vanished Summers

Vanished Summers, passed and gone,
Here find resurrection.—
Each crowned corn-head closely filled,
Packed and pressed with suns distilled
Into lively sap which throws
Rays of sunlight as it grows.—
These enchanted, waving tall
Golden ears contain them all:
All the long delightful days,
When June met us face to face;
Light and laughing grace re-born
In great fields of upright corn.—
Earth's tremendous charity
Full-accomplished here we see
Who gives us for familiar food
The lovely lilt of July's mood.—
One minute, brown husk contains
Summer's shadow, Autumn rains,
Spring's delicious wayward green,
Even Winter's pallid, lean
Blood of mingled frost and snows
Virtue on our sheaves bestows.
So to give us daily bread
The very sky's transfiguréd.

MARGARET SACKVILLE (1881-1963)

Hay-Making
from *The Seasons*

Now swarms the village o'er the jovial mead:
The rustic youth, brown with meridian toil,
Healthful and strong, full as the summer rose;
Blown by prevailing suns, the ruddy maid,
Half-naked, swelling on the sight, and all
Her kindled graces burning o'er her cheek.
Ev'n stooping age is here; and infant hands
Trail the long rake, or, with the fragrant load,
O'er-charged, amid the kind oppression roll.
Wide flies the tedded grain; all in a row,
Advancing broad, or wheeling round the field,
They spread the breathing harvest to the sun,
That throws refreshful round a rural smell:
Or, as they rake the green appearing ground,
And drive the dusky wave along the mead,
The russet hay-cock rises thick behind,
In order gay; while heard from dale to dale,
Working the breeze resounds the blended voice
Of happy labour, love, and social glee.

JAMES THOMSON (1700-1748)

from *Seasons*

Oh the shouting Harvest-weeks!
   Mother Earth grown fat with sheaves;
Thrifty gleaner finds who seeks;
   Russet-golden pomp of leaves
Crowns the woods, to fall at length;
   Bracing winds are felt to stir,
Ocean gathers up her strength,
   Beasts renew their dwindled fur.

CHRISTINA ROSSETTI (1830-1894)

from *The Seasons*

The sun has lost his rage; his downward orb
Shoots nothing now, but animating warmth,
And vital lustre; that, with various ray,
Lights up the clouds, those beauteous robes of heav'n,
Incessant roll'd into romantic shapes,
The dream of waking fancy! broad below
Cover'd with ripening fruits, and swelling fast
Into the perfect year, the pregnant earth
And all her tribes rejoice.

JAMES THOMSON (1700-1748)

My Father's Fields

Not all the sights your boasted garden yields,
Are half so lovely as my father's fields,
Where large increase has bless'd the fruitful plain,
And we with joy behold the swelling grain!
Whose heavy ears, toward the earth reclin'd,
Wave, nod, and tremble to the whisking wind.

MARY LEAPOR (1722-1746)

A Day Born of the Gentle South

After dark vapours have oppress'd our plains
For a long dreary season, comes a day
Born of the gentle South, and clears away
From the sick heavens all unseemly stains.
The anxious month, relievèd of its pains,
Takes as a long-lost right the feel of May;
The eyelids with the passing coolness play
Make rose-leaves with the drip of Summer rains.
The calmest thoughts come round us; as of leaves
Budding—fruit ripening in stillness—Autumn suns,
Smiling at eve upon the quiet sheaves—. . .
Sweet Sappho's cheek—a smiling infant's breath—
The gradual sand that through an hour-glass runs—
A woodland ruvulet—a Poet's death.

JOHN KEATS (1795-1821)

October
from *The Months*

On frosty morns with the woods aflame, down, down
The golden spoils fall thick from the chestnut crown.
May Autumn in tranquil glory her riches spend,
With mellow apples her orchard-branches bend.

ROBERT BRIDGES (1844-1930)

from *The Lotos-Eaters*

Lo! sweetened with the summer light,
The full-juiced apple, waxing over-mellow,
Drops in a silent autumn night.
All its allotted length of days,
The flower ripens in its place,
Ripens and fades, and falls, and hath no toil,
Fast rooted in the fruitful soil.

ALFRED, LORD TENNYSON (1809-1892)

from *A Year's Windfalls*

In brisk wind of September
  The heavy-headed fruits
Shake upon their bending boughs
  And drop from the shoots;
Some glow golden in the sun,
  Some show green and streaked,
Some set forth a purple bloom,
  Some blush rosy-cheeked.

CHRISTINA ROSSETTI (1830-1894)

Martins: September

At secret daybreak they had met—
Chill mist beneath the welling light
Screening the marshes green and wet—
An ardent legion wild for flight.

Each preened and sleeked an arrowlike wing,
Then eager throats with lapsing cries
Praising whatever fate might bring—
Cold wave, or Africa's paradise.

Unventured, trackless leagues of air,
England's sweet summer narrowing on
Her lovely pastures; nought they care—
Only this ardour to be gone.

A tiny, elflike, ecstatic host . . .
And I neath them, on the highway's crust,
Like some small mute belated ghost,
A sparrow pecking in the dust.

WALTER DE LA MARE (1873-1956)

Bright Autumn

I met not any friend abroad
But swallows, stirring to depart;
And my old shadow skimmed the road,
Happy without a heart.

Whether from those cold sunlit lands,
Or from the unimagined sky—
Blessed by some spirit's secret hands,
I drew the breath of sudden joy.

From all or from myself alone,
I asked not, being wise again;
But oh, the silver pastures shone,
And were translated then . . .

Fall not, soul, from those grave heights!
Look, to-day is bright with sun.
Hold back that fear; the darkest nights
See dawn, and soon are done.

FRANK KENDON (20th century)

Evening

Spare and like honey is the clovery texture
Of evening at pasture, the glint hush of summer
Falling in hueless folds,
Trailing at the horizon a cool hem;
Evening intact yet tremulous with far clamour
Of calling ewes and lambs—
Could love but fracture
One bone-grey sun-ray between dreamer
And dreamer!—
Calling until the wold's
Dun waters close invisibly over them.

LILIAN BOWES LYON (1895-1949)

These Fields at Evening

They wear their evening light as women wear
  Their pale, proud beauty for a lover's sake,
Too quiet-hearted evermore to care
  For moving worlds and musics that they make.
And they are hushed as lonely women are,
  So lost in dreams they have no thought to mark
How the wide heavens blossom, star by star,
  And the slow dusk is deepening to the dark.

The moon comes like a lover from the hill,
  Leaning across the twilight and the trees,
And finds them grave and beautiful and still,
  And wearing always, on such nights as these,
A glimmer less than any ghostly light,
  As women wear their beauty in the night.

DAVID MORTON (1886-1911)

from *To Autumn*

O Autumn, laden with fruit, and stainèd
With the blood of the grape, pass not, but sit
Beneath my shady roof; there thou may'st rest
And tune thy jolly voice to my fresh pipe,
And all the daughters of the year shall dance!
Sing now the lusty song of fruits and flowers . . .

. . . 'The Spirits of the Air live on the smells
Of fruit; and Joy, with pinions light, roves round
The gardens, or sits singing in the trees,'
Thus sang the jolly Autumn as he sat;
Then rose, girded himself, and o'er the bleak
Hills fled from our sight; but left his golden load.

WILLIAM BLAKE (1757-1827)

from *Strange Fruit*

This year the grain is heavy-ripe;
The apple shows a ruddier stripe;
Never berries so profuse
Blackened with so sweet a juice
On brambly hedges, summer-dyed.
The yellow leaves begin to glide;
But Earth in careless lap-ful treasures
Pledge of over-brimming measures,
As if some rich unwonted zest
Stirred prodigal within her breast . . .

LAURENCE BINYON (1869-1943)

Cock-Pheasant

Gilded with leaf-thick paint; a steady
Eye fixed like a ruby rock;
Across the cidrous banks of autumn
Swaggers the stamping pheasant-cock.

The thrusting nut and bursting apple
Accompany his jointed walk,
The creviced pumpkin and the marrow
Bend to his path on melting stalk.

Sure as an Inca priest or devil,
Feathers stroking down the corn,
He blinks the lively dust of daylight,
Blind to the hunter's powder-horn.

For me, alike, this flushed October—
Ripe, and round-fleshed, and bellyful—
Fevers me fast but cannot fright, though
Each dropped leaf shows the winter's skull.

LAURIE LEE (b 1914)

The Pheasant

Cock stubble-searching pheasant, delicate
Stepper, Cathayan bird, you fire
The landscape, as across the hollow lyre
Quick fingers burn the moment: call your mate
From the deep woods tonight, for your surprised
Metallic summons answers me like wire
Thrilling with messages, and I cannot wait
To catch its evening import, half-surmised.
Others may speak these things, but you alone
Fear never noise, make the damp thickets ring
With your assertions, set the afternoon
Alight with coloured pride. Your image glows
At autumn's centre—bright, unquestioning
Exotic bird, haunter of autumn hedgerows.

SIDNEY KEYES (1922-1943)

103

Autumnal Threads

'Twas when the fields had shed their golden grain
And burning suns had scar'd the russet plain;
No more the rose or hyacinth were seen,
Nor yellow cowslip on the tufted green:
But the rude thistle rear'd its hoary crown,
And the ripe nettle shew'd an irksome brown.
In mournful plight the tarnish'd groves appear,
And nature weeps for the declining year:
The sun, too quickly, reach'd the western sky,
And rising vapours hid his ev'ning eye:
Autumnal threads around the branches flew,
While the dry stubble drank the falling dew.

MARY LEAPOR (1722-1746)

The Latter Rain

The latter rain,—it falls in anxious haste
Upon the sun-dried fields and branches bare,
Loosening with searching drops the rigid waste,
As if it would each root's lost strength repair;
But not a blade grow green as in the spring,
No swelling twig puts forth its thickening leaves;
The robins only mid the harvests sing,
Pecking the grain that scatters from the sheaves:
The rain falls still,—the fruit all ripened drops,
It pierces chestnut burr and walnut shell,
The furrowed fields disclose the yellow crops,
Each bursting pod of talents used can tell,
And all that once received the early rain
Declare to man it was not sent in vain.

JONES VERY (1813-1880)

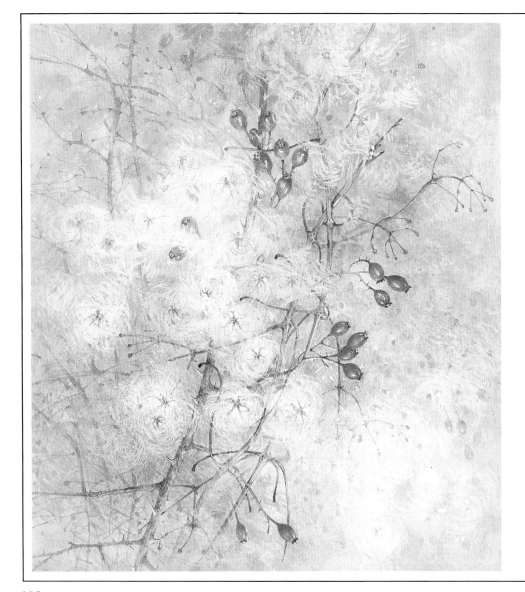

from *Wilderness*

The blackthorns hung with clinging sloes
Blue-veiled in weather coming cold,
And ruby-tasselled shepherd's-rose
Where flock the finches plumed with gold,
And swarming brambles laden still
Though boys and wasps have ate their fill.

EDMUND BLUNDEN (1896-1974)

Traveller's Joy

Through the valley and over the down
The withering hedge bends dry and brown,
The sycamore leaves hang rent and seared,
And the Traveller's Joy is Old Man's Beard—
Up the marsh and over the lea
The milk-white gulls sail up from the sea—
And it's O for the wind and the weeping rain,
And the summers that never shall rise again
Whatever may come to be.

ROSAMUND MARRIOTT WATSON (1863-1911)

from *Seed-Time*

Flowers of the willow-herb are wool;
Flowers of the briar berries red;
Speeding their seed as the breeze may rule,
Flowers of the thistle loosen the thread.
Flowers of the clematis drip in beard,
Slack from the fir-tree youngly climbed;
Chaplets in air, flies foliage seared;
Heeled upon earth, lie clusters rimed.

Now seems none but the spider lord;
Star in circle his web waits prey,
Silvering bush-mounds, blue brushing sward;
Slow runs the hour, swift flits the ray.
Now to his thread-shroud is he nigh,
Nigh to the tangle where wings are sealed,
He who frolicked the jewelled fly;
All is adroop on the down and the weald.

Verily now is our season of seed,
Now in our Autumn; and Earth discerns
Them that have served her in them that can read,
Glassing, where under the surface she burns,
Quick at her wheel, while the fuel, decay,
Brightens the fire of renewal: and we?
Death is the word of a bovine day,
Know you the breast of the springing To-be.

GEORGE MEREDITH (1828-1909)

St Luke's Summer

Now is the tolling time
Between the falling and the buried leaf;
A solitary bell
Saddens the soft air with the last knell
Of summer.
Gone is the swallow's flight, the curving sheaf;
The plums are bruised that hung from a bent bough,
Wasp-plundered apples in the dew-drenched grass
Lie rotting now.
Doomed with the rest, the daggered hawthorn bleeds
Bright crimson beads
For the birds' feast.
Gone are the clusters of ripe cherries,
Tart crabs and damsons where a bullfinch tarried,
Only the camp-fire coloured rowan berries
Blaze on.
Now is the time of slow, mist-hindered dawns,
Of sun that stains
Weeds tarnished early in the chilling rains,
Of coarse-cut stubble fields
Where starlings gather, busy with the scant grain,
And with hoarse chattering proclaim
The spent season.
Now are the last days of warm sun
That fires the rusted bracken on the hill,
And mellows the deserted trees
Where the last leaves cling, sapless, shrunk, and yellow.

A robin finds some warm October bough
Recapturing his song
Of Aprils gone,
And tardy blackbirds in the late-green larch
Remember March.

PHOEBE HESKETH (b 1909)

from *North Wind in October*

In the golden glade the chestnuts are fallen all;
From the sered boughs of the oak the acorns fall:
The beech scatters her ruddy fire;
The lime hath stripped to the cold,
And standeth naked above her yellow attire:
The larch thinneth her spire
To lay the ways of the wood with cloth of gold.

   Out of the golden green and white
Of the brake the fir-trees stand upright
In the forest of flame, and wave aloft
To the blue of heaven their blue-green tuftings soft.

ROBERT BRIDGES (1844-1930)

A Windy Day

This wind brings all dead things to life,
Branches that lash the air like whips
And dead leaves rolling in a hurry
Or peering in a rabbits' bury
Or trying to push down a tree;
Gates that fly open to the wind
And close again behind,
And fields that are a flowing sea
And make the cattle look like ships;
Straws glistening and stiff
Lying on air as on a shelf
And pond that leaps to leave itself;
And feathers too that rise and float,
Each feather changed into a bird,
And line-hung sheets that crack and strain;
Even the sun-greened coat,
That through so many winds has served,
The scarecrow struggles to put on again.

ANDREW YOUNG (1885-1971)

110

Autumn

Therefore their latter journey to the grave
Was like those days of later autumn tide
When he who in some town may chance to bide
Opens the window for the balmy air,
And seeing the golden hazy sky so fair,
And from some city garden hearing still
The wheeling rooks the air with music fill,
Sweet hopeful music, thinketh: Is this Spring?
Surely the year can scarce be perishing?
But then he leaves the clamour of the town,
And sees the scanty withered leaves fall down,
The half-ploughed field, the flowerless garden plot,
The dark full stream by summer long forgot,
The tangled hedges where, relaxed and dead,
The twining plants their withered berries shed,
And feels therewith the treachery of the sun,
And knows the pleasant time is well nigh done.

WILLIAM MORRIS (1834-1896)

November

The mellow year is hasting to its close;
The little birds have almost sung their last,
Their small notes twitter in the dreary blast—
That shrill-piped harbinger of early snows:
The patient beauty of the scentless rose,
Oft with the Morn's hoar crystal quaintly glass'd,
Hangs, a pale mourner for the summer past,
And makes a little summer where it grows:
In the chill sunbeam of the faint brief day
The dusky waters shudder as they shine,
The russet leaves obstruct the straggling way
Of oozy brooks, which no deep banks define,
And the gaunt woods, in ragged, scant array,
Wrap their old limbs with sombre ivy twine.

HARTLEY COLERIDGE (1796-1849)

The Last Week in October

The trees are undressing, and fling in many places—
On the gray road, the roof, the window-sill—
Their radiant robes and ribbons and yellow laces;
A leaf each second so is flung at will,
Here, there, another and another, still and still.

A spider's web has caught one while downcoming,
That stays there dangling when the rest pass on;
Like a suspended criminal hangs he, murmuring
In golden garb, while one yet green, high yon,
Trembles, as fearing such a fate for himself anon.

THOMAS HARDY (1840-1928)

from *The Storm is Over*

But ah! the leaves of summer that lie on the ground!
What havoc! The laughing timbrels of June,
That curtained the birds' cradles, and screened their song,
That sheltered the cooing doves at noon,
Of airy fans the delicate throng,—
Torn and scattered around:
Far out afield they lie,
In the watery furrows die,
In grassy pools of the flood they sink and drown,
Green-golden, orange, vermilion, golden and brown,
The high year's flaunting crown
Shattered and trampled down.

ROBERT BRIDGES (1844-1930)

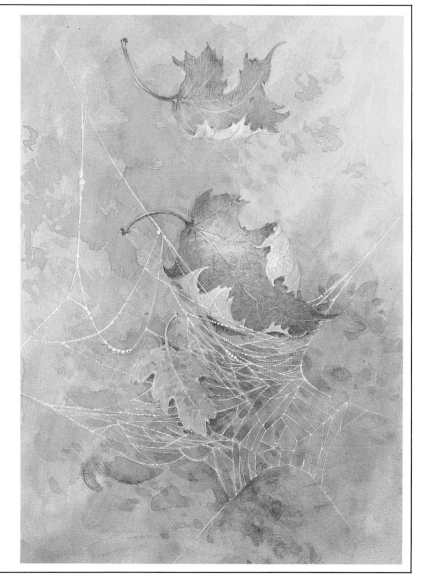

Last Hours

A gray day and quiet,
   With slow clouds of gray,
And in dull air a cloud that falls, falls
      All day.

   The naked and stiff branches
    Of oak, elm, thorn,
In the cold light are like men aged and
      Forlorn.

   Only a gray sky,
    Grass, trees, grass again,
And all the air a cloud that drips, drips,
      All day.

   Lovely the lonely
    Bare trees and green grass—
Lovelier now the last hours of slow winter
      Slowly pass.

JOHN FREEMAN (1880-1929)

November Skies

Than these November skies
Is no sky lovelier. The clouds are deep;
Into their gray the subtle spies
Of colour creep,
Changing that high austerity to delight,
Till even the leaden interfolds are bright.
And, where the cloud breaks, faint far azure peers
Ere a thin flushing cloud again
Shuts up that loveliness, or shares.
The huge great clouds move slowly, gently, as
Reluctant the quick sun should shine in vain,
Holding in bright caprice their rain.
And when of colours none,
Not rose, nor amber, nor the scarce late green,
Is truly seen,—
In all the myriad gray,
In silver height and dusky deep, remain
The loveliest,
Faint purple flushes of the unvanquished sun.

JOHN FREEMAN (1880-1929)

November Night

Listen.
With faint-dry sound,
Like steps of passing ghosts,
The leaves, frost-crisp'd, break from the trees
And fall.

ADELAIDE CRAPSEY (1878-1914)

What is Winter?

What is winter? A word,
A figure, a clever guess.
That time-word does not answer to
This drowsy wakefulness.
The secret stream scorns the interval
Though the calendar shouts one from the wall;
The spirit has no last days;
And death is no more dead than this
Flower-haunted haze.

EDMUND BLUNDEN (1896-1974)

Reluctance

Out through the fields and the woods
  And over the walls I have wended;
I have climbed the hills of view
  And looked at the world, and descended;
I have come by the highway home,
  And lo, it is ended.

The leaves are all dead on the ground,
  Save those that the oak is keeping
To ravel them one by one
  And let them go scraping and creeping
Out over the crusted snow,
  When others are sleeping.

And the dead leaves lie huddled and still,
  No longer blown hither and thither;
The last lone aster is gone;
  The flowers of the witch-hazel wither;
The heart is still aching to seek,
  But the feet question 'Whither?'

Ah, when to the heart of man
  Was it ever less than a treason
To go with the drift of things,
  To yield with a grace to reason,
And bow and accept the end
  Of a love or a season?

ROBERT FROST (1874-1963)

119

Christmas

I had almost forgotten the singing in the streets,
Snow piled up by the houses, drifting
Underneath the door into the warm room,
Firelight, lamplight, the little lame cat
Dreaming in soft sleep on the hearth, mother dozing,
Waiting for Christmas to come, the boys and me
Trudging over blanket fields waving lanterns to the sky.
I had almost forgotten the smell, the feel of it all,
The coming back home, with girls laughing like stars,
Their cheeks, holly berries, me kissing one,
Silent-tongued, soberly, by the long church wall;
Then back to the kitchen table, supper on the white cloth,
Cheese, bread, the home-made wine;
Symbols of the night's joy, a holy feast.
And I wonder now, years gone, mother gone,
The boys and girls scattered, drifted away with the snowflakes,
Lamplight done, firelight over,
If the sounds of our singing in the streets are still there,
Those old tunes, still praising;
And now, a life-time of Decembers away from it all,
A branch of remembering holly spears my cheeks,
And I think it may be so;
Yes, I believe it may be so.

LEONARD CLARK (1905-1981)

Holly

'Tis a brave tree. While round its boughs in vain
The warring wind of January bites and girds,
It holds the clusters of its crimson grain,
A winter pasture for the shivering birds.
Oh, patient holly, that the children love,
No need for thee of smooth blue skies above:
Oh, green strong holly, shine amid the frost;
Thou dost not lose one leaf for sunshine lost.

AUGUSTA WEBSTER (1837-1894)

from *The Setting Sun*

Then comes the Winter, like a hale old man
Wrapped in his cloak with frosty locks and beard.
Winter is the time for clear cold starlight nights,
And driving snows, and frozen roads and rivers,
For crowding round the blazing Christmas fire,
For telling tales that make the blood run cold,
For sipping elder-wine and cracking filberts,
For friendships, chilblains, fun, roast beef, mince pies,
And shivering fits on jumping into bed:
And thus the year goes round, and round, and round.

JAMES HURNARD (late 19th-early 20th century)

121

Blow, Blow, Thou Winter Wind

from *As You Like It*

Blow, blow, thou winter wind,
Thou are not so unkind
  As man's ingratitude;
Thy tooth is not so keen,
Because thou art not seen,
  Although thy breath be rude.

Heigh ho! sing, heigh ho! unto the green holly:
Most friendship is feigning, most loving mere folly:
  Then, heigh ho, the holly!
  This life is most jolly.

Freeze, freeze, thou bitter sky,
That dost not bite so nigh
  As benefits forgot:
Though thou the waters warp,
Thy sting is not so sharp
  As friend remembered not.

Heigh ho! sing, heigh ho! &c.

WILLIAM SHAKESPEARE (1564-1616)

from *The Task*

Now stir the fire, and close the shutters fast,
Let fall the curtains, wheel the sofa round,
And, while the bubbling and loud-hissing urn
Throws up a steamy column, and the cups,
That cheer but not inebriate, wait on each,
So let us welcome peaceful evening in . . .

  Oh Winter, ruler of th'inverted year, . . .
I love thee, all unlovely as thou seem'st,
And dreaded as thou art. Thou hold'st the sun
A prisoner in the yet undawning east,
Shortening his journey between morn and noon,
And hurrying him, impatient of his stay,
Down to the rosy west; but kindly still
Compensating his loss with added hours
Of social converse and instructive ease,
And gathering, at short notice, in one group
The family dispersed, and fixing thought,
Not less dispersed by day-light and its cares.
I crown thee king of intimate delights,
Fire-side enjoyments, home-born happiness,
And all the comforts that the lowly roof
Of undisturbed retirement and the hours
Of long uninterrupted evening know.

WILLIAM COWPER (1731-1800)

from *Frost at Midnight*

Therefore all seasons shall be sweet to thee,
Whether the summer clothe the general earth
With greenness, or the redbreast sit and sing
Betwixt the tufts of snow on the bare branch
Of mossy apple-tree, while the nigh thatch
Smokes in the sun-thaw; whether the eave-drops fall
Heard only in the trances of the blast,
Or if the secret ministry of frost
Shall hang them up in silent icicles,
Quietly shining to the quiet Moon.

SAMUEL TAYLOR COLERIDGE (1772-1834)